EDGE BOOKS

All About Dogs

YORKSHIRE TERRIERS

by Tammy Gagne

Consultant: Jennifer White
Bricriu Kennels and
President, My Prissy Paws, Inc.

Capstone press
Mankato, Minnesota

Edge Books are published by Capstone Press,
151 Good Counsel Drive, P.O. Box 669, Mankato, Minnesota 56002.
www.capstonepress.com

Copyright © 2010 by Capstone Press, a Capstone Publishers company.
All rights reserved.
No part of this publication may be reproduced in whole or in part,
or stored in a retrieval system, or transmitted in any form or by any means,
electronic, mechanical, photocopying, recording, or otherwise, without
written permission of the publisher.
For information regarding permission, write to Capstone Press,
151 Good Counsel Drive, P.O. Box 669, Dept. R, Mankato, Minnesota 56002.
Printed in the United States of America

 Books published by Capstone Press are manufactured with paper containing at least 10 percent post-consumer waste.

Library of Congress Cataloging-in-Publication Data
Gagne, Tammy.
　Yorkshire terriers / by Tammy Gagne.
　　p. cm. — (Edge Books. All about dogs)
　Includes bibliographical references and index.
　Summary: "Describes the history, physical features, temperament, and care of the Yorkshire terrier breed" — Provided by publisher.
　ISBN 978-1-4296-3362-8 (library binding)
　1. Yorkshire terrier — Juvenile literature. I. Title. II. Series.
SF429.Y6G34 2010
636.76 — dc22　　　　　　　　　　　　　　　　　　　　2008055555

Editorial Credits
Jennifer Besel and Molly Kolpin, editors; Veronica Bianchini, designer;
　Marcie Spence, media researcher

Photo Credits
Art Resource, N.Y./Fine Art Photographic Library, London, 9
Capstone Press/Karon Dubke, cover, 1, 12, 13 (bottom), 15, 17, 18, 19, 21, 24, 27
Courtesy of Jennifer White, 16
iStockphoto/cynoclub, 25, 29
Mary Evans Picture Library/Illustrated London News Ltd., 13 (top)
Peter Arnold/Biosphoto/Klein J.-L. & Hubert M.-L., 6
Photo by Fiona Green, 5, 22, 28
Private Collection/Ken Welsh/The Bridgeman Art Library, 10–11
Shutterstock/Dee Hunter, 7

Table of Contents

A Big Dog in a Small Body 4

Yorkie History 8

Small but Spunky 14

Caring for a Yorkshire Terrier 20

Glossary 30

Read More 31

Internet Sites 31

Index 32

CHAPTER 1

A Big Dog in a Small Body

The Yorkshire terrier is among the world's smallest dog breeds. Everything about this dog is tiny, except its attitude. Yorkies, as they are commonly called, usually weigh less than 7 pounds (3 kilograms). But few Yorkies seem to realize how small they are. Yorkies are known to stand up to dogs several times their size.

Yorkshire terriers make great pets for people who live in small homes or apartments. These dogs take up little space and need only minimal exercise. A Yorkie can even be trained to use a litter box.

Owners can take their tiny Yorkies almost anywhere. Many owners carry their dogs in tote bags specially made to hold small dogs. You might have passed a Yorkie with its owner without realizing it.

Yorkies are some of the smallest dogs in the world.

EDGE FACT

A Yorkshire terrier named Sylvia holds the record for being the smallest dog in history. Sylvia weighed just 4 ounces (113 grams).

Is a Yorkie Right for You?

Yorkies get along well with most other pets. Cats and other dogs make wonderful companions for this breed. Yorkies have a strong hunting instinct, though. If you have pets like mice and rats, a Yorkie isn't a good fit for your home.

Other pets must understand that the Yorkie is boss. A Yorkie might try to keep other pets away from its toys or food. It might also growl at larger pets when they don't do what the Yorkie wants.

Training is the key to a well-behaved Yorkie.

For a healthy puppy, go to a respected breeder.

Many pet shops sell Yorkie puppies. However, the best way to find a puppy is through a **breeder**. Responsible breeders choose only the best dogs for their breeding programs. These dogs are likely to produce healthy, friendly puppies. Yorkies can also be adopted from animal shelters or rescue groups. Rescue groups help place unwanted dogs in new homes.

breeder — someone who breeds and raises dogs or other animals

CHAPTER 2

YORKIE HISTORY

Yorkshire terriers are named for the area in England where the breed began. In the mid-1800s, many Scottish people moved to England and brought their dogs with them. Breeders in Yorkshire developed the Scottish dogs into the Yorkshire terrier breed. Ancestors of the Yorkie probably include the Clydesdale and Paisley terriers.

During the 1800s, Yorkshire terriers usually lived with working-class people and business owners. Yorkies helped their human friends by catching rats in **textile** mills and coal mines. These early, hardworking Yorkies were a bit larger than modern Yorkshire terriers.

Until the last half of the 1800s, the Yorkshire terrier was known as the toy terrier or the broken-haired Scotch terrier. During the 1870s, English breeders began entering their Yorkies in dog shows. Soon the breed took on its official name as the Yorkshire terrier.

textile — a fabric or cloth that has been woven or knitted

Early Yorkies were useful pets for working-class people.

EDGE FACT

During the 1800s, many weavers owned Yorkies. People often joked that the weavers spun their dogs' silky coats on the looms.

Yorkies in America

As the Yorkie became more popular in England, it also won the hearts of visiting Americans. It wasn't long before the Yorkshire terrier made its way to the United States. In 1872, the first recorded American Yorkshire terrier was born. The American Kennel Club (AKC) accepted the Yorkshire terrier as an official breed in 1885.

It is likely that many Yorkshire terriers were used to keep American factories free of rats. But by the early 1900s, dog shows were becoming more popular around the world. Americans started to value Yorkies more as show dogs and pets than as hunters.

Early Yorkies were put to work, keeping cotton mills like this one free of rats.

A Breed Standard

The Yorkshire Terrier Club of England formed in 1898. The purpose of the club was to create a **breed standard**. Lady Edith Wyndham-Dawson was the club's secretary. She was one of the first breeders to develop the Yorkshire terrier we know today. A woman named Miss Palmer helped Lady Wyndham-Dawson care for the Yorkies she bred.

Lady Wyndham-Dawson left for Ireland during World War I (1914–1918). Miss Palmer then went to work for another well-known Yorkie breeder, Mrs. Crookshank. The champion dogs bred by these women are the ancestors of many modern Yorkies.

breed standard — the physical features of a breed that judges look for in a dog show

Yorkies in the late 1800s were bred to have long, sleek coats.

CHAPTER 3

Small But Spunky

The first thing most people notice about Yorkshire terriers is their tiny size. But although they weigh just a few pounds, these canines shouldn't be underestimated. Yorkies do nearly all the things larger dogs do.

Physical Features

Most terriers are part of the AKC's terrier group. Because of their size, though, Yorkies belong to the toy dog group. Belonging to the toy group doesn't mean that Yorkies can be treated like toys. The name "toy" just means that a breed is especially small. Most of today's Yorkshire terriers weigh between 4 and 7 pounds (2 and 3 kilograms).

A Yorkshire terrier's head is small. Its eyes are dark. They often seem to sparkle, giving the breed an intelligent expression. The ears are V-shaped and stand upright. A Yorkie's nose is black.

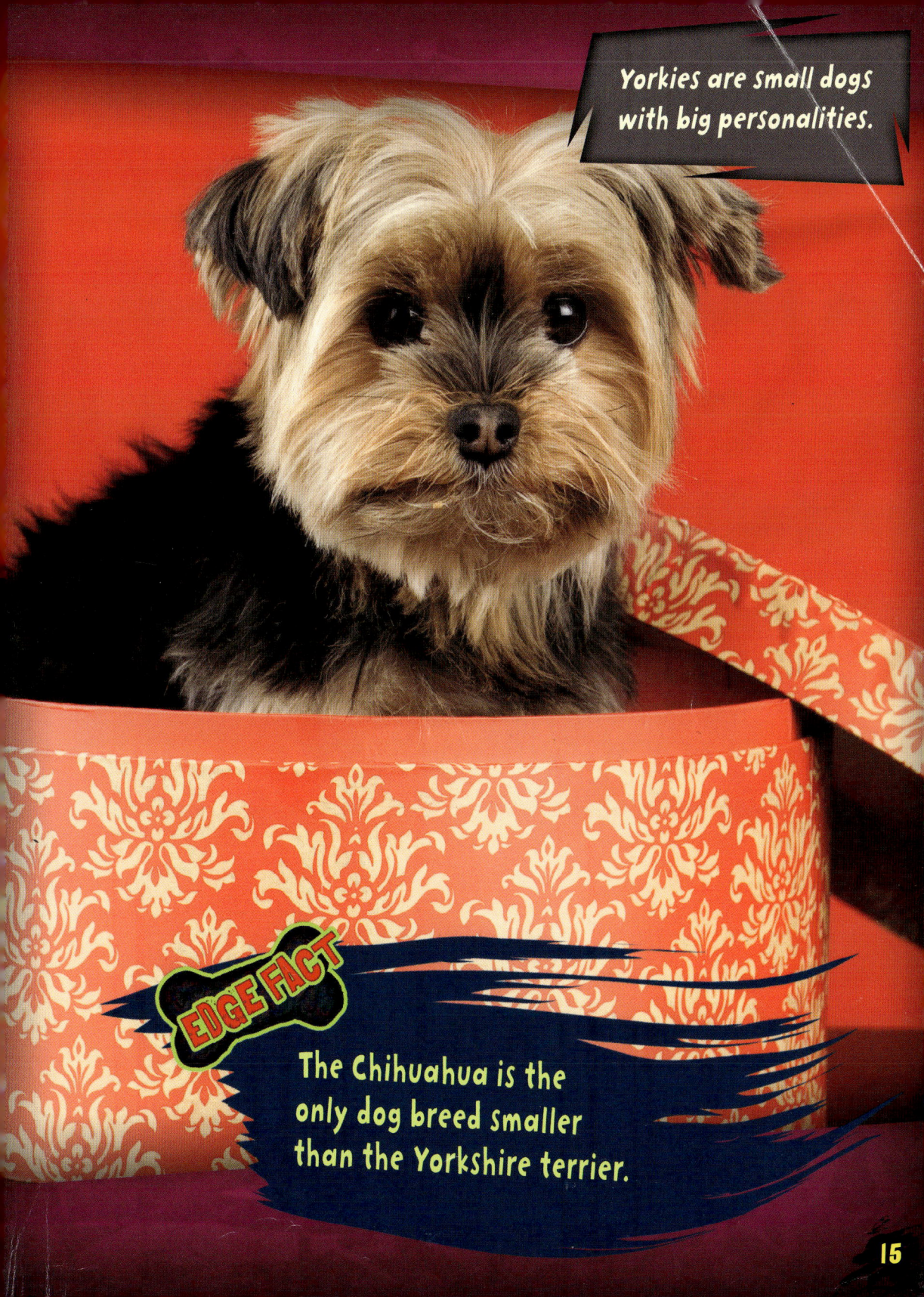

Yorkies that go to dog shows have long hair that reaches the floor.

A Colorful Coat

The hair on Yorkshire terriers is straight and long. Their silky hair shines and feels very soft. A show dog's hair reaches the floor. Yorkies that don't compete in shows usually sport a shorter hairstyle called a pet clip.

The Yorkie's unusual coloring makes the dog stand out from other breeds. Yorkies have blue and tan coats. The blue is a dark, steel-blue color. This blue color covers the dog's body from the back of its neck to its tail. Tan hairs are found on the dog's head, chest, ears, and legs.

Short Tails

In the United States, most Yorkshire terriers' tails are docked. The breeder cuts away part of a puppy's tail soon after it is born. Tails were originally docked to keep hunting dogs from getting caught in brush. Docking also helped keep the area around the dog's tail clean.

Today Yorkies' tails are docked mostly because of tradition. In many European countries, docking is illegal because it is thought to be cruel. Some people think that docking will eventually be outlawed in the United States as well. For now, though, a Yorkshire terrier competing in AKC dog shows must have a docked tail.

Most Yorkies in the United States have docked tails.

Temperament

More people own Yorkies than any other type of terrier. Yorkies have charming personalities. They seem to love everyone. This breed of dog makes an ideal pet for families with older children. But these tiny dogs need to be handled gently. Young children may not know how to treat a small dog. Families need to make sure their tiny dog is protected.

Despite their small size, Yorkies are incredibly brave. They are also especially loyal to the people they love. A Yorkie will quickly jump between its owner and any threat. Because they are so fearless, Yorkshire terriers make excellent watchdogs. A Yorkie is usually the first to announce the arrival of visitors.

Yorkies form strong bonds with their human family members.

CHAPTER 4

Caring for a Yorkshire Terrier

Yorkshire terriers may be small, but they need just as much care as bigger dogs. Yorkies must be well trained. To make sure their Yorkies remain friendly, owners should **socialize** their dogs. Yorkies also need regular exercise and grooming.

Training

Some Yorkshire terriers seem to have a stubborn streak. Owners can teach their Yorkies to become more obedient through training. Training should begin immediately after bringing your Yorkie home. During each training session, repeat the commands you have already taught your pet. This repetition will help your Yorkie remember what it has learned.

socialize — to train to get along with people and other dogs

Owners need to work with their dogs every day to teach them good behavior.

Feeding your Yorkie two or three small meals a day will help keep it healthy.

EDGE FACT

If you feed your Yorkie dry dog food, be sure the pieces are small enough for its tiny mouth.

Feeding

Yorkshire terriers must eat their meals on time. If a small dog goes too long without eating, it can suffer from a condition called **hypoglycemia**. Owners can prevent this problem by feeding Yorkies two or three smaller meals instead of one large meal each day.

Feed your Yorkie a high-quality dog food. Dogs need food made from lean meats and vegetables rich in vitamins. Healthy food helps keep their bodies strong and fit. High-quality dog foods can be found at most pet supply stores. These foods are more expensive than supermarket brands, but they are worth the added cost.

Because Yorkshire terriers are so small, they eat only a small amount of food each day. Large dogs may eat several cups of food. But toy breeds usually eat less than one cup.

hypoglycemia — low blood sugar

Exercise

The Yorkie's size makes it easy for owners to carry their dogs places. But small dogs need exercise and enjoy walking on leashes just as much as bigger ones.

Even though they love and need to move, these tiny dogs can't exercise for long periods of time. On a long hike, you may need to carry your Yorkie for part of the trip.

A long walk is great exercise for your dog.

Even though they're small, Yorkies can compete in agility contests.

Some Yorkies get exercise by competing in organized events. Agility is a fun sport in which dogs race over ramps and other equipment. Although Yorkies are small, they are surprisingly sturdy.

Other Yorkies compete in Earthdog events. In these contests, a small animal like a rat is placed in a cage at the end of a tunnel. Dogs run through the underground maze of tunnels to reach the rat as quickly as possible.

Grooming

A Yorkie owner's most important grooming tool is a brush. A Yorkie's fine hair needs daily brushing to remove dirt and dead hair from its coat. Brushing also keeps the hair from tangling.

Yorkies that compete in shows must have long hair. Many owners keep a Yorkie's long hair out of its eyes by using elastic bows. A Yorkie competing in a dog show must have its hair tied back in one or two bows.

Whether your Yorkie has long or short hair, it needs regular baths. Yorkies with short hair need baths once every few weeks. Yorkies with long hair need to be bathed weekly. Regular bathing also helps prevent skin infections.

You'll need to trim your Yorkie's nails every few weeks. Overgrown nails can catch on clothing and carpeting. They can also make walking painful.

Brush your Yorkie's teeth every day. Because toy breeds have very small mouths, their teeth are often crowded. This creates many hard-to-reach areas where plaque and tartar can build up. Remember to only use products made for dogs on your Yorkshire terrier. Products made for people can harm your pet.

Brushing a Yorkie's coat every day helps keep it clean and shiny.

Health Care

A Yorkshire terrier should visit a veterinarian at least once each year. After your Yorkie reaches age 7, it should see the vet twice a year.

During a checkup, your pet will receive any necessary **vaccinations**. The vet will also check your dog's joints. Some Yorkies suffer from a problem called patellar luxation. Yorkies with this problem have a kneecap that has slipped out of place. Dogs sometimes need surgery to correct this problem.

Vet checkups are an important part of taking care of your Yorkie.

vaccination — a shot of medicine that protects animals from a disease

One way to keep your Yorkie healthy is by having your vet spay or neuter it. These simple operations help control the pet population by preventing dogs from having puppies. Dogs that are spayed or neutered have a lower risk for many diseases, including cancer.

Caring for a Yorkshire terrier can be a demanding job, but it comes with many rewards. By providing your dog with top-notch care, you help it stay happy and healthy. In return, your Yorkie will give you many years of love and companionship.

EDGE FACT

Yorkies have long life spans. Some Yorkies live well into their teens.

Glossary

breed (BREED) — a certain kind of animal within an animal group; breed also means to mate and raise a certain kind of animal.

breeder (BREE-duhr) — someone who breeds and raises dogs or other animals

breed standard (BREED STAN-derd) — the physical features of a breed that judges look for in a dog show

hypoglycemia (hye-poh-glye-SEE-mee-uh) — the medical term for low blood sugar

neuter (NOO-tur) — a veterinary operation that prevents a male dog from producing offspring

patellar luxation (puh-TEL-ur luhk-SAY-shuhn) — a condition in which the kneecap slips out of place

socialize (SOH-shuh-lize) — to train to get along with people and other dogs

spay (SPEY) — a veterinary operation that prevents a female dog from producing offspring

textile (TEK-stile) — a fabric or cloth that has been woven or knitted

vaccination (vak-suh-NAY-shun) — a shot of medicine that protects animals from a disease

Read More

Fetty, Margaret. *Yorkshire Terrier: Tiny but Tough*. Little Dogs Rock! New York: Bearport, 2009.

Gray, Susan H. *Yorkshire Terriers*. Domestic Dogs. Chanhassen, Minn.: Child's World, 2007.

Green, Sara. *Yorkshire Terriers*. Dog Breeds. Minneapolis: Bellwether Media, 2009.

Internet Sites

FactHound offers a safe, fun way to find Internet sites related to this book. All of the sites on FactHound have been researched by our staff.

Here's all you do:

Visit *www.facthound.com*

FactHound will fetch the best sites for you!

Index

adoption, 7
American Kennel Club
   (AKC), 10, 14, 17
appearance
   coats, 9, 13, 16, 26
   colors, 16
   ears, 14, 16
   eyes, 14
   size, 4, 5, 14, 15, 18, 20, 25
   tails, 16, 17

breeders, 7, 17
breed history
   in England, 8, 12
   and jobs, 8, 11
   in the United States, 10–11

exercising, 4, 20, 24–25

feeding, 22, 23

grooming, 20, 26, 27

life span, 29

personality. *See* temperament
puppies, 7, 17, 29

temperament, 4, 6, 15, 18, 19, 20
training, 4, 6, 20, 21

veterinary care, 28–29

Yorkshire terriers